Papa,

Tell Me Another Story

Papa,

Tell Me Another Story

Read the exciting true-life stories of "Yankee Boy"

Written by Ralph "Yankee" Arnold
Edited by Jay Kominsky
Artwork by Cheryl Detwiler Mihalka

XULON PRESS ELITE

Xulon Press Elite
2301 Lucien Way #415
Maitland, FL 32751
407.339.4217
www.xulonpress.com

Printed in the United States of America.

Paperback ISBN-13: 978-1-6628-1517-1
Ebook ISBN-13: 978-1-6628-1518-8

Papa, Tell Me Another Story
By
YANKEE

Telling stories to children and adults has been not only a joy of mine, but also a great part of my ministry over the last sixty-plus years. Although all the stories were harmless for children, I would often watch the adults cringe in disbelief when they realized where the story was going. Of course, the children would sit there in total awe as I spun the story and watched as their eyes bugged out and their mouths flung open. As a safety precaution, perhaps parents should read the stories first to see what they would deem appropriate. I hope you enjoy.

Table of Contents

Introduction and Dedication

To Abby Arnold

The actual picture of Abby asking me to tell her another story.

When I was about seventy years of age, Grandma Betty and I went to Athens, Georgia to spend some time with our son, Eddie Arnold, his wife, Deborah, and their two children, Jordan and Abby. While eating at

Cracker Barrel in Commerce, Georgia, Abby climbed into my lap and asked me to tell her some stories about when I was a little boy. Being only eight years old, she was very inquisitive as to what my life was like when I was young, but she also wanted me to tell her some of the crazy things that happened to me. After about four or five interesting little stories she looked at me and said, "Papa, you need to write a book."

I said, "If I ever do, I'll dedicate it to you."

Right before her fifteenth birthday, she reminded me about my promise to write a book in her honor, and the time has now come. Here are a few of my stories. Although all of them are true, you may not find them totally appropriate for your small sons or daughters to hear, so please feel free to pick and choose the ones you believe will be acceptable.

I was not privileged to know any of my grandparents. My dad's name was Ralph Arnold, and he was thirty-one years old when he married my mother, Doris McElhannon, who was only fourteen years old. None of these stories are meant to shame my parents or to be critical, in any way, about the way I was raised. These were hard times, and I believe my mother and father did the best they could with the knowledge that they had. They could not lead me where they had never been, and they could not teach me what they did not know.

It is also very important to know that many of the stories happened when I was very young. When I was a child I thought as a child. My perspective of what really happened is being recorded as I remember them, and verified by my mother, brother, and sisters. In some cases, I may have embellished a few stories to produce color, humor, and perhaps a storyline for a teachable moment.

Abby is now sweet sixteen, goes to Athens Christian School, and loves her family and the Lord Jesus Christ.

Dr. Ralph "Yankee" Arnold

I placed my faith in Jesus Christ as my Savior when I was eighteen years old. It happened in the living room of Raymond Jackson, my father-in-law. Mr. Jackson encouraged me to read the Bible, beginning with the Gospel of John. Frustrated after reading the first three chapters, Mr. Jackson sat down and clearly explained John 3:16 to me. I stated, "If what John 3:16 says is true, then I know I am going to hell." This troubled me so much that I began weeping as my father-in-law explained how to be saved. Mr. Jackson shared the gospel: that Jesus Christ died for me, was buried, and rose again to pay for all of my sins, and that by believing in Christ I would have everlasting life. That day, I did exactly what the Bible said to do to be saved… I believed in Christ alone. Raymond Jackson is the only person who has personally asked me about the greatest thing a anyone could know—that being **how to get to Heaven.**

My favorite verse in the Bible, next to Ephesians 2:8-9, is John 14:31: "But that the world may know that I love the Father..." The backbone for my ministry has been my wonderful, godly, sacrificial, and dedicated wife, Betty, to whom I've been married for over sixty years. This ministry has resulted in countless thousands of people choosing to trust in Christ as their Savior. Without her I would have no ministry. I've had no regrets in my life of service to the Lord. I wouldn't change my life for anyone else's life in the world. The Lord has been true to his promise in Psalm 37:4: "Delight thyself in the Lord; and he shall give thee the desires of thine heart."

How Did I Get the Name of Yankee?

❖

I believe an explanation of my name, Yankee, is in order, as so many testimonies in this book refer to that name. I will begin with a brief introduction to my family. My mother and father have both died, and I have every intention of honoring my parents with nothing but the truths that they shared with me, and publicly shared with all.

My father, Ralph Arnold, went by the nickname "Shine," which he earned by selling moonshine from his liquor stills. My mother had six children by the time she was twenty-three. I was the third. My mother and dad were both rebels from Georgia. None of the six children were born in the hospital, because we all chose to be born at home so that we could be near our mother.

At this time in our country, people were coming out of the Great Depression and did whatever they could to scratch out a living. My dad dug wells, cut hair, made moonshine, and made a little counterfeit money. He also made many trips to the jailhouse for being drunk and spent time on the chain gang. At other times, he was running from the law. One of those trips took him and my mother to Rimersburg, Pennsylvania, where I was born on February 4, 1942.

When I was old enough to understand, my mother informed me (and all who would listen) how I got my name, "Yankee." She said that when I was born, I had long, straight, black hair all over my body, including sideburns, and hair going down my back. My dad said, "That's the ugliest kid I have ever seen in my life," and that I "looked like a monkey." My father wanted to put me into a burlap sack and throw me into the river, but my mother would not let him. A Dr. Wilson came a little later to the house, looked at me, looked at my dad, and said, "Looks just like his daddy, doesn't he?" This is when my daddy called me a "Blankety-blank Yankee." So, I have been called Yankee since the day I was born. My mother always referred to me as "Yankee Boy."

My mother swore that every word of this is the truth. She did say, however, that she did not totally agree with my dad; I was ugly, just not "that ugly."

About six months later we moved back to Georgia. I was a Yankee raised in the South and have been shot at from both sides most of my life. So, now you know the rest of the story.

No Prayer, Bible, or Church Was in Our Family Life

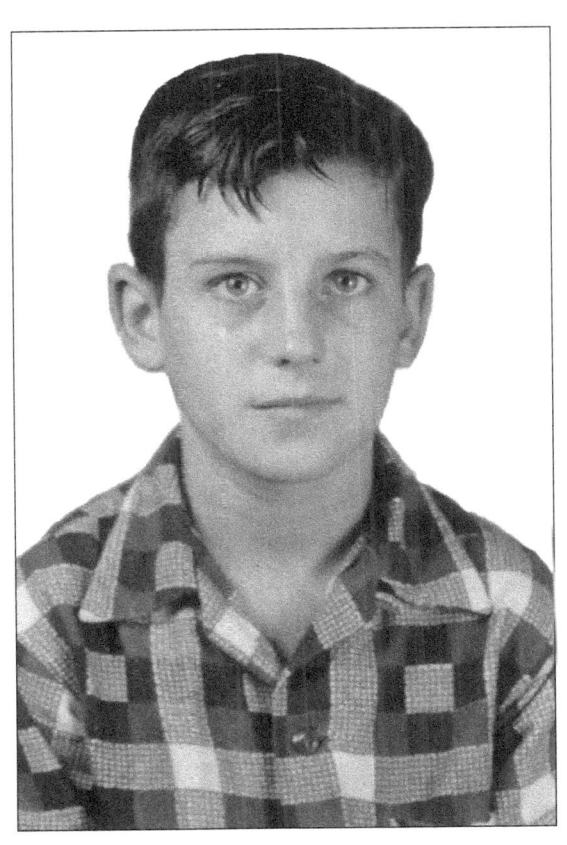

STORIES OF YANKEE BOY

I have no recollection of ever seeing my mother and father in church during my childhood years, nor did I ever see them read the Bible, own a Bible, or ever talk about the Bible. My parents never talked about God, Jesus Christ, or heaven and hell in our home. There was never a prayer during any meals or bedtimes. I never once ever heard the words, "I love you."

It's very difficult for many people to believe that you could live in good old Christian America and never learn anything about the Lord. I now understand that it would be most difficult for my parents to teach me things they did not know. Perhaps no one ever told my mother and father about the wonderful love of Jesus Christ.

In later years, many referred to our family as "hillbillies," but the truth of the matter was that we came from the "Flatwoods" between Lexington and Rayle, Georgia. Since many of my relatives lived deep in the wooded country rather than in the cities, it was easy for them to be involved in liquor stills.

My dad had polio when he was a child. It affected his right foot, which was turned completely to the right. It caused him to walk with a limp. He had five brothers and two sisters, and I had the privilege of leading Aunt Grace and Aunt Sue to the Lord when they were both about seventy years old. By the time I came to know the Lord, and learned how to clearly explain the gospel, my dad's brothers had all passed away.

My mom and dad with Lizzie and Net.

There was a time when my mother and father moved to Florida, leaving me with my Uncle John, and my two older sisters (Lizzy and Net) with Uncle Jimmy Lane. As three little children, we had no knowledge of where our parents were or how long they had been gone. I didn't see my sisters for a long time. I will never forget seeing them for the first time after so many months. We stood in the middle of the dirt road, and hugged each other, and cried. I cannot recall how long it was before my parents came back to Georgia.

I believe it is truly amazing that although I did not grow up in a Christian environment, I had a deep burning desire to know the Lord. I shared many things with my mother, later in life, about what I remembered when I was young. She would say, "Yankee, you were only about two years old when that happened."

The Day I Cut Off the Dog's Tail

I was very young, very innocent, and very naïve as to the seriousness of my deeds. It all began one afternoon when my older sister Annette, known simply as "Net," proceeded to lead her innocent little brother into a serious crime.

Net and Me

She approached me and said, "Yankee, let's play house." I said that I didn't know how to play house. She simply said that I would be the daddy and she would be the mommy. We played around in the yard for a little while, and then she told me that she was hungry. I told her that I was, too. I asked her what we were going to eat, and she said, "Hot dogs." I actually thought we were just pretending, but I asked her where we were going to get hot dogs. She said, "From the dog."

Well, that made perfect sense, because I really didn't know where hot dogs came from. Now, I knew. She told me to get my dog, and when I did she backed him up to this log with his tail hanging over it. She then told me to go and get the ax. As I was only about five or six years old, I had a most difficult time dragging this double-bladed ax to the log. I put the long handle way underneath my arm. It took me two hands to lift the ax. When she told me to chop off my dog's tail at the right place, I simply dropped the ax, which quickly brought a loud hollering from my dog. His tail dropped to the left of the log onto the ground.

My dog took off running around the house. Net did not say anything, as I recall, but went through the front door of the house. I very nonchalantly walked around the house to the back porch. There sat my mother, peeling pota-toes. Wouldn't you know it, at that very moment, while I'm standing there looking at my mother, my whimpering little dog walked by. Then I heard my mother proclaim with a loud, screaming voice, "Oh my God, what happened to the dog?"

As if on cue, my sweet, beloved sister stepped out of the house onto the porch and very calmly said, "Yankee cut his tail off." I thought my mother was going to end my life. She beat me until I could not sit down. If you're wondering what happened to my sister Net... absolutely nothing. I do believe, at this point, that I am supposed to give a moral to this story. If there is one, I have not found it after seventy years. I want you to know that I did love my dog, and never had a desire to hurt my dog. My dog still loved me.

Where did *you* think hot dogs really come from?

Why I Don't Like Meatloaf

W hen you have six children in the family, and only your mother as a means of support, you don't always have all the food you want to eat. My mother did the best she could, but I was a growing boy and always hungry. My Aunt Eileen and Uncle Merle had moved their travel trailer right beside our little house where we lived in Wegley, Pennsylvania. We looked upon them as rich people because they had so much more than we had.

Many times, after school, I would run home from the bus stop to beat my older sisters to the house. I knew we did not have much to eat. I also knew that my aunt's travel trailer had a refrigerator. In that refrigerator would usually be something I could eat without her knowing it.

On several occasions, when my aunt and uncle were not home, I would check their refrigerator because I had once found a can of potted meat and made a sandwich. I could spread it quickly, eat my sandwich, and get out of the trailer before anyone else got home. I had found my own private stash.

After several weeks of this, my aunt got all of us children together and lined us up outside of her trailer. She told us that she didn't know which one of us had been going into the trailer and eating the dog food, but if she found out she was going to blister someone's little rear end so that they couldn't sit down. I knew at this point I was not eating potted meat, or meat loaf, but dog food. I did not admit to doing this dastardly deed, but I never did it again. To this day, I have never had a great desire to eat meatloaf because it reminded me so much of the dog food. Even to this day I very seldom eat meatloaf unless I can totally baptize it in catsup.

There Was a Moonshiner in the Choir

Having his own liquor still, and with all the white lightning he could drink, I very seldom saw my dad sober. When he was sober, he was fairly good, but when he was drunk he was pretty mean. To a little child, it's easier to recall the bad memories than the good ones. When sober, my dad was pretty ingenious. I rode with him several times in his Model T truck. He would go to the sawmill, get slabs left over from pine trees, and take them to a neighbor's home.

Once there, he would jack up the right rear wheel of the truck, which was solid rubber, put a big wideband belt on the back tire, and attach it to a saw blade about ten or fifteen feet from the rear of the truck. He used the motor from the truck to turn the saw blade and ran the wood slabs on a tabletop to cut them down into two-inch strips. He sold these strips as stove wood for cooking.

My two older sisters and I rode many a night in the back of that Model T truck, while my daddy drove home drunk after being at some neighbor's home. I remember us huddled together because we were so cold. While driving home over those old dirt roads, it seemed that he hit every bump and rode in and out of every rut. My dad seemed to be oblivious to our suffering and would joyfully sing at the top of his lungs. It appeared that the drunker he was the better he sang. It is true that people would come from miles around just to sit and listen to my daddy sing.

Between Lexington and Raile, Georgia, stood the old Bethesda Methodist Church. On occasion, when my dad was feeling the spirits, he would drop by this little old white church. Immediately, they would work on my dad to join them in the choir even though he was drunk. Like I said: the drunker he was, the better he could sing.

My mother and my aunt Grace filled in many of the blanks in my memory. By the way, my daddy is buried in the cemetery behind this little Methodist Church. If my dad ever knew anything about the Lord, no one remembers him ever sharing that with the family.

He Looks Like a Monkey

———— ❖ ————

Well, Net set me up again. This was an unusual day, for scarcely do I remember my dad bringing a stranger into our home to eat supper. We had a long wooden table with wooden benches on both sides for the kids to sit on. My mom sat on the end to the left, and my dad sat at the end of the table to my right. I never really like sitting that close to my dad, but it was not my choice. I don't remember what we ate, but most days it was rabbit stew, which I truly loved.

One afternoon my dad brought a friend of his to our home and asked him to stay for supper. The other kids across the table from me simply slid down and made room for our visitor. Believe it or not, I only met this man this one day, but I still remember his name, though I dare not use it in this story for fear he may have some relatives that may want to have a word with me. My sister Net was sitting beside me to my left. After a few moments, she leaned over to me and whispered, "Yankee, look at that man. He sure is ugly." I nodded my head in agreement and laughed.

My dad was not pleased with this behavior at the table, so he asked me what I was laughing about. I replied, "Nothing."

After a few moments Net leaned over to me and whispered again, so that my dad couldn't hear. "Yankee, look at him. He looks like a monkey." I quickly looked at him and agreed, shook my head up and down, and laughed very loudly.

My father raised his voice and said, "What are you laughing about?" I knew by the tone of his voice that I would have to give an answer. Remember, I was only about six years old. I was not yet skilled in the art of lying effectively. How would I tell my dad, who was sitting within arm's length, why I was laughing? As the years have since gone by, I've been told that it's always better to tell the truth. As I sit here contemplating this story, over seventy years later, I am not convinced that it's always better. Perhaps it is better to say nothing.

Without hesitation, and without understanding the seriousness of the situation, nor the danger that lay ahead, I looked at my dad and quickly repeated what my beloved sister had told me. Pointing to his friend, I said, "He looks like a monkey."

In a flash, my dad sent me into the twilight zone. His left arm swung to his left, and the back of his hand caught me upside the head, knocking me off the bench and into the wall by the stove. He then took me out of the house and, with a piece of stove wood, proceeded to take my life. Oh, by the way—if you're wondering what happened to Net, the answer was simple… nothing! I never figured out how my sister, who was only about a year and a half older than me, was able to outsmart me so many times, and get away with it. She was either brilliant or I was stupid. I never saw that man again.

A Jug of Milk in the Middle of the Road

O ne day, my dad was sober and planned to do a little yardwork. This was rare. It was very hot outside. My mother needed some milk, so my dad asked Net and me to go down this dirt road to a neighbor's home about a half mile away. The neighbor owned some milk cows, and our family, quite often, would get a gallon of milk from them. But this was the first time that only my sister and I would go to get the milk. A gallon of milk was too heavy for one of us to accomplish this task, which is why my dad sent both of us. On the way we were able to play, skip, and eat a few may-pops that grew along the road. Now, if you have never eaten may-pops, you've really missed out. Of course, we just picked the yellow ones, knocked the dust off, and ate the insides. Boy, were they good.

About halfway to the neighbors' house was a crossroad. We walked across it and journeyed up a hill. We reached the neighbors, gave them the money my dad said to pay for the jug of milk, and began our journey back to the house.

This was a big jug. It had two little loops on the sides so we could both put our fingers in and drag the milk between us. This was working pretty well until we got about halfway back to the crossroad. That was when my sister had another brilliant idea. She said, "Yankee, if you can drag the milk to the middle of the crossroad, I will drag it the rest of the way home." I might have been young, and maybe even a little stupid, but I was not that stupid. I could see that I was closer to the crossroad than she would be for the rest of the way home.

I quickly agreed, put a finger in each one of those little loops on the side of the jug, and gladly dragged that milk between my legs. While I sweated under the heavy load; Net hummed, and skipped, ate some may-pops, and had a pretty good time. But I did it; I made it to the middle of the crossroad.

With great joy, and much delight, I informed my beloved
sister that it was her turn to drag the milk the rest of the
way home. But without missing a beat, she quickly said
that she was not going to do it. I told her that she'd promised. She said she didn't care, and she wasn't going to do it.

23

Knowing that I was in the right, and that I had nothing to fear, I informed her that I was going to go and tell Daddy because I knew she was really in trouble. Leaving the jug of milk in the middle of the crossroad, I took off running to the house to tell Daddy what Net had done. The one thing I forgot was that my sister could outrun me. She got to Daddy first and told him that I would not help her bring the milk home. When I got to the house, Daddy was waiting for me with a nice sized stick in his hand. He proceeded to beat the tar out of me and told me to go back and help my sister bring the milk home.

If you are wondering if Net ever received a whooping for all those things she did to her precious, innocent little brother, the answer is… no.

Three Little White Kids
Picking Cotton

Lizzie, Yankee Boy, and Net

I will never forget the time my mother needed a little extra money, so she loaned my two older sisters and me to a farmer down the road who needed some cotton pickers. We would place a big old white sheet on the fairly level ground and put the cotton that we picked in a pile on the sheet. The owner was hoping to get about 100 pounds of cotton from us three little children.

Liz was about nine years old, Net about seven, and I about five and a half to six. Using children to pick the cotton wasn't a normal practice, but the owner was trying to help out my mom. As I looked out across those white fields all I could see was many black folks bending over and picking cotton.

They would hum or sing, but I never knew what it was. I did not have to bend over because the cotton was at my eye level. The trick was to get the cotton without those prickly little barbs sticking your fingers. My two sisters did a pretty good job, but I don't recall ever finishing one side of one row. The cotton sack around my neck was difficult to even drag along on the ground. We kids never received anything for picking the cotton, but we did manage to make enough for my mom to get some new glasses.

The Day My Doggie Left Home

I suppose every little boy wants and loves a little dog. I was no different. The first little dog I remember having was named Pal, because I considered him to be my pal, my friend. Little did I know that when I left the yard one day, my little dog would follow me down to the highway. I turned around just in time to see him running across the road as a Greyhound bus ran over him. The bus never stopped. I stood there, totally brokenhearted.

A couple of years later I got another little dog. I don't recall his name, but we had lots of fun as he chased me around the yard.

One day I picked him up with my two hands under his two front legs and looked at him eye to eye. I extended my arms straight up in the air and pretended to drop him without my hands ever leaving his body. My dog seemed to enjoy this, appearing to give me what I interpreted to be a doggy smile. I then threw him higher and caught him under both of his front legs.

I proceeded to toss him considerably higher than before, but when he came back down, he slid right through my hands and hit the ground. He got up, staggered a little bit, and ran off into the woods. I never saw my dog again. How could I have done such a terrible thing? It had never occurred to me that I might drop him. Since that dreadful moment, I have watched a great number of men and women take their darling little babies, toss them into the air, and catch them just like I did with my little dog.

I cringe thinking what they would go through if they accidentally dropped that precious loved one. I've never witnessed someone dropping their child, but I cannot understand why they would run the risk.

I'm Going to Africa

❖

In 1959 my mother took all six of us children to live in Wegley, Pennsylvania. Because she did not have the means to support six children, she was informed by social service people that we would be put into foster homes. Two of my sisters, Net and Sybil, were willing to live with my Aunt Eileen and Uncle Merle in Franklin, Virginia. This decision kept us from being placed in foster homes. After two years, my oldest sister, Liz, and I volunteered to go to Franklin for the next two years. Liz returned home after a year, and I remained in Franklin for one more year.

I was pretty much a quiet kid, and I did not make friends in school very easily. Without my sister there I got bored and very lonesome. My aunt and uncle loved to fish, and they felt blessed, and very thrilled, to have me to paddle the boat for them. I was promised a quarter for every bass caught over three pounds.

One day we were on our way to the river so that they could fish while I paddled the boat. As I sat in the back of the car,

I once again drowned myself in self-pity. What was I going to do with my life? I continued to complain to my aunt and uncle and talked about running away to Africa. They didn't respond but continued the drive to the river. They could hear my low murmuring about how bored I was.

Suddenly, my uncle pulled to the right of the road, stopped the car, and told me to get out. I quickly did so without any hesitation, and without a word. They said nothing. I watched as they drove off toward the river.

I really did not know where Africa was or how I would get there. This was in the middle of the summer. I had no water, or sandwiches, or knowledge of which way to go. I was sure that they had simply driven out of sight, and that after a few minutes they would realize the error of their ways, feel sorry for the way they treated me, and come back and get me. But after standing in the hot sun for a while, hungry and thirsty, I decided to walk back to their house. I began to hope that every car that passed me, regardless of which way it was going, would be my aunt and uncle. It had never occurred to me how many miles we were from home. I walked and walked and walked until the sun went down, and it was evening when I finally got to the back door of their house.

I had been humbled and humiliated because of my pride. I wanted to go in the house, but at the same time I didn't want to go in. I slowly opened the door, and there sat my aunt and uncle at the kitchen table about to eat some fresh fish with hush puppies. As I walked in they never said a word, but when I looked at the table I saw that they had my plate and a glass of iced tea waiting for me. I learned that, regardless of what I may be thinking, I must be careful of what I say.

I never did get to Africa.

The Bogeyman Tried to Get Me

For this Georgia boy, now living in Pennsylvania, the dead of winter was no piece of cake. We had a coal fired furnace in the basement of our two-room house. Because the coal truck could not get up the road, the driver would simply dump a load of coal at the end of our property. Guess who had to carry the coal up to the house and shovel it through an outside window into the furnace room?

Since I was the oldest boy, stoking the furnace became my job. Putting coal into the basement was not as difficult for me as putting coal into the furnace. Let me explain. My mother would always say, "Yankee boy, go downstairs and stoke the furnace." This simply meant that I had to move this big iron bar to open up the stove, break up large clumps of coal, stir it around, and put the pieces of coal into the furnace. I had no problem with this during the day because there was a little window that let light into the furnace room. At night, however, there was only a little light bulb hanging from the ceiling by the electrical wire with a string for me to pull. That one little light at night was not very bright, and it left a lot of shadows all around.

There were many places for the bogeymen to hide.

I knew that one day they were going to get me. Every night when I had to load the furnace, my soul was flooded with fear. But I did it. I was smart enough to leave the upstairs door open so that the light from the living room would shine down the stairs and partially across the basement room. I would then dart in to the furnace room and hit that light string within seconds. I knew I was fast, probably faster than any kid in the world. I could turn out the downstairs light in the furnace room, go through the doorway, run through the basement room, and make it to the top of the stairs before the bulb went dark. If there was a bogeyman lurking in the dark he would definitely have to be fast in order to catch me.

Remember my sister, Net? She would wait at the top of the stairs for me to come flying around to the bottom of the basement stairs. When she heard me coming, she quickly turned off the light and closed the upstairs door so there was absolutely no light anywhere, leaving me totally unarmed in the midst of at least a dozen bogeymen. In the darkness, I had to climb the stairs slowly. Bogeyman were grabbing under every step trying to get my feet. As I yelled for my sister to open the door, I could hear her laughing on the other side. I cannot believe my sister did this to me. Only when my mother hollered at Net did she finally open the upstairs door. I was never so happy. Once again, I had escaped with my life from the clutches of the bogeyman.

No, Net did not get a whooping.

The Scariest Night of My Life

I t is only natural for children to have some scary moments in their lives. I sure had my share. It does not help when you sit around at night telling scary stories.

One night as we were doing just that, we saw the bedroom door slowly open. A hand reached for the light switch turned it off, and quickly closed the door. My two older sisters ran to the door, but there was no one in the house but us. This only fuel the fire of our fear, until we were so scared that we had a difficult time going to sleep. We did not have nightlights in our home, so when it was dark it was *very* dark.

That same night, when I awoke, I was afraid to open my eyes because I heard something at the foot of the bed. I knew it was the bogeyman. I was afraid to move because I knew he would grab me. When I slowly opened my eyes, I could barely see. But there, standing in the corner by the door, stood a man. My mother and stepdad were in the other room sound asleep. My younger brother and four sisters were all asleep. I was the only one that could alert my family to this devastating dilemma. I seriously considered screaming as loud as I could. That would cause my mother to hear me and come running, or else cause the man in the corner to quickly leave my room.

I was paralyzed with fear. If I moved or said anything, he would get me. I laid there for several hours watching him standing in the corner, unable to see any of his features. I figured if he started toward me, I would really scream. You will never know how excited I was to see morning light coming into my room, because the man in the corner was slowly revealed. That excitement gave way to devastation when I realized I had gone through such fear for several hours in the middle of the night all because of my coat, sitting on the top of a broom handle that stood in the corner.

Daddy Promised to Shoot Santa Claus

To appreciate this story, you must remember that I was not raised in a Christian home or a Christian environment. As a child, what I believed about Santa Claus had to be the truth. Although I never heard about heaven or hell at this stage of my life, I did understand that I must be good for Santa Claus to bring me presents on Christmas day. I had absolutely no knowledge that this day was set apart as a holy day for the birth of Jesus Christ.

For the first several years that I can remember, I never received any presents except one little red tractor with black wheels that was no larger than, perhaps, six inches in length. I do recall that sometimes there would be a bowl of apples, oranges, and various kinds of nuts for all of us as a family, but there were no personal gifts. Then one year, Liz, Net, and I decided to have a talk with our dad about this Christmas thing. It was hard for us to believe that other kids were so much better than we were, especially when we were told that the better you were the more gifts you would receive. I will never forget that day because my dad was sober, and he promised us that year would be different. We were going to have the best Christmas, with the most toys that anyone has ever received.

Without any remorse, my dad assured us that when Santa Claus passed over our house, he was going to shoot him and bring us all the toys that Santa had for everyone else. Taking my dad at his word, we truly believed it with all our hearts.

Later, we three children got an ax and went into the woods near our house. There we found just the right pine tree, cut it down, and dragged it to the house. We took two, short one-by-four-inch boards, made an "X" with them, and nailed them to the bottom of the tree. For decorations, we made icicles from the silver linings of the Prince Albert tobacco cans our dad left all over the yard. I never saw my dad smoke cigarettes that were purchased in a pack; he always rolled his own. You never saw such happy, excited, and joyful kids as we waited for Christmas Day. We did not see our dad the day before Christmas because he was already celebrating in the spirits called white lightning.

On Christmas morning we could not wait to look under the tree and see all those presents that we knew we deserved because we had been so good. To our dismay, our hearts sunk when we saw nothing there. My mom told us that our dad was outside leaning against a tree. As we approached him, I believe it was Lizzie that asked him what happened. My dad was drunk, but he was not that drunk—he remembered what he had promised us. We could see that he really felt bad. He told us that he was waiting outside until Santa Claus came over. He told us how he shot at Santa Claus but missed.

I know that it would be hard for others to believe that we would buy into his story, but we did. None of us felt sorry that Santa Claus would be dead, or that other kids would never have another Christmas. If only my dad could shoot straight.

King for a Night

When does a boy start liking girls? Well, l remember being deeply in love when I was in the first grade. Well, I liked her a lot, anyway. Can you believe that after seventy years I still remember Glenda's name? In those days, most of the boys wore overalls and went barefooted unless it was too cold.

The school in Lexington, Georgia, was going to have a king and queen night, to which the public was invited. This was, I suppose, about the year 1948. There was to be a king and queen that would represent each class in the school. The class chose my secret sweetheart to be the queen. I then developed an overwhelming desire to be the king. I just could not think of my girlfriend walking down the aisle with another boy. I was totally enraged with jealousy.

When the vote was taken as to who would represent our class as the king, another boy was chosen. I was heartbroken, but there was nothing I could do. Then, about a week before the prom, the teacher announced to the class that the boy chosen to be the king was not going to be able to attend. I don't believe the reason was ever given, but for a moment this did give me hope. The class voted again, and would you believe it? I was chosen to be the king. You can imagine how excited I was. I would get to walk in as the king, with the queen, in front of everybody.

I was told that I would have to be dressed up and wear shoes for this great occasion. Several days passed without any action from my mom and dad to buy me new clothes. My mom told me that my dad had sold some chickens and was going to take me to the store to buy me some new clothes, and he did. I got the clothes. Later that day, my dad took me to a store a couple of miles east of Lexington to buy me some shoes. My dad and I got out of the Model T and headed toward the store. My dad went inside ahead of me. Before I could go inside, my dad came running back out—more hopping than running because of his right foot, damaged by polio when he was a child. He ducked quickly into a cornfield, running for his life because the owner of the store was shooting at him. I never did understand why, but at that moment the only thing I knew to do was to follow my dad through the cornfield. I could hear the gun going off as we ran to the other side of the field.

Once we knew that we were safe, my dad showed me a bullet hole in his pant leg, but he was not injured. Needless to say, there was no time left to find or buy me shoes because the dance was that night. I was so proud to put on my new pants, new shirt, and a new belt, and to be able to walk down the aisle with the queen. As I recall, I was the only person there who was still barefooted.

After being married to Betty for over thirty years we decided to see this girl Glenda who I liked very much during the first and second grade at the Lexington Elementary School. It was kind of strange walking up to her door and asking her if she remembered me. It was kind of humbling to find out that she never did like me, nor did she know my name. I never did like humble pie.

Kay, I'll Make You Look Pretty

K ay was my third sister, and she was about a year and a half younger than me. Now, these next few statements are not meant to be derogatory, hurtful, or hateful in any way toward my sister Kay. This was common knowledge to everyone, especially to Kay. Kay knew that Liz and Net were a lot prettier than she was. Their hair was long, wavy, and beautiful, and Kay's hair was short and straight.

Being her big brother, it really hurt me to hear Kay continually talk about how ugly she was, and that she wished she was pretty like Liz and Net. Kay tried many times to roll her hair or get a permanent so that it wouldn't look so straight, but nothing worked. I saw her cry many times, but nothing I said brought much comfort to her.

Some of the boys in my grade liked to have a butch haircut. It meant that your hair was very short. The trick was to get the short hairs on the top of your head to stand straight up. They came out with some kind of gunk to put on your hair that would hold it in place. When I finally let my hair grow long, I used this gunk to put some waves in my hair. It worked pretty well. In the morning I could use the gunk, comb my hair, and have it look like a very natural wave. So, one day, while feeling very sorry for my sister Kay, I came up with a great idea. I said. "Kay, I am going to make you pretty."

She looked at me, with almost tears in her eyes, and she said, "Yankee, really?"

I said, "Yes, but you gotta do exactly what I say." She trusted me, and agreed, and was willing to do anything to look pretty. I just knew this was going to work.

I told Kay to put this gunk all over her hair, and then roll it in little perks all over her head. She immediately obeyed. I told her that when she went to bed, she should lay in one position all night, so as not to disturb any of the little curls held down by bobby pins, and tomorrow she would be the prettiest girl in school. But the next morning began the most frightful day of her life. It did not take long for Kay to realize that she had not lain still without moving her head. When Kay looked into the mirror, she was horrified.

Most of the bobby pins had fallen out of her hair. Her hair had been left standing as straight as a stick all over her head.

Remember Alfalfa of the "Little Rascals"? He always had a cowlick (a few long hairs standing straight up in the air), and Kay looked like a cow had licked her whole head. She was unable to get her hair to lie down or form a wave.

47

Kay did not go to school that day. I was so sorry for Kay, and felt so bad that my little scheme did not work. The good Lord knows that I tried. As the years have rolled by, my sister Net went to be with the Lord when she was sixty-two, and my sister Liz went to be with the Lord when she was sixty-eight. Kay has now outlived them both. I can honestly say that the older Kay grew, the sweeter, and prettier, she became.

Yankee Has a Book in His Pants

Lizzie and her dancing partner, Nancy, entered many school jitterbugging competitions. They were good and they knew it, and so did everybody else. They would rather dance than eat. Often times, when Lizzie would come in late at night, later than she was supposed to, my stepdad would threaten her under penalty of death!

I'll never forget this one night: before Lizzie left to go to a dance, my mom and stepdad warned her that if she wasn't in by eleven o'clock, she would be beaten within an inch of her life. We older kids wondered what Lizzie was going to do.

There was a standing rule at home. If you got a whipping in school, you would get one when you got home. Well, that day I was taken to the boiler room by my schoolteacher, Mr. Pellegrin. I knew what was going to happen to me that night when my mom and dad found out that I had been paddled in school. I'm not sure how they found out, but I lived in fear and trembling waiting for the moment that the whipping would happen that night. I had to wait until my stepdad was in the right mood. When eleven o'clock came, and Lizzie wasn't home, none of us kids wanted to go to bed. We wanted to see what was going to happen to Lizzie. By now my stepdad was getting into the whipping mood.

When Lizzie finally came home, she had no good reason for staying out late; she just wanted to. Liz and I were about to get the beatings of our lives, on the same night, at the same time. I should not have told Lizzie what I was going to do, but I was so proud of myself for thinking of this great idea that I just had to tell her.

I'd put a book in the back of my pants.

When my stepdad grabbed me by my left arm and proceeded to murder me, I jumped up and down and hollered at the top of my lungs. My acting ability was second to none. He then let go of me and grabbed my sister. She jumped up and down and all around the room, while my stepdad blistered her backside, and I could not help but laugh out loud at how smart I was, and how foolish she was for not doing the same thing with a book. However, my acting career was short lived, because my sister, who took offense at my laughter, informed my stepdad what I had done. My sister got her quick revenge.

There was one thing I just had to know about Liz, so I asked her. If she knew she was going to get a whipping if she stayed out too late, why did she do it? She said, "Yankee, I think about the whipping that I'm going to receive, which will last a few minutes, and I think about the dancing that I enjoyed for three or four hours. In my mind, the joy of dancing outweighs the pain of my spanking. Therefore, I do it." Everything seemed to be so logical in her mind, but it scared me to death to think like that.

Yankee Goes to the
Boiler Room

I knew the day would come when I would get to enter junior high school. I was excited and amazed that I had made it this far, but I was also very fearful. You see, my two older sisters, Net and Liz, had already had an encounter with a particular homeroom teacher by the name of Mr. Pellegrin. They shared with me how, on many occasions, disruptive students were sent to the boiler room to be paddled. This paddle was made of wood, with about two rows of quarter-inch drilled holes in one end. It wasn't the only thing used for discipline. On one occasion, both sisters came home with welts on the back of their legs and buttocks from being whipped with a rubber hose.

I determined that one thing I would not do was to be disruptive, in any way, in Mr. Pellegrin's class. I would be the best student he ever had. The semester moved along fairly well until one day when Mr. Pellegrin stepped out of the classroom and said he would be back in a moment. Nick, who was sitting in the back of the room, decided to make a paper airplane. I looked over and saw what he was doing, but I did not know that he was going to sail that paper airplane from the back of the classroom to the front. The class saw the plane sail through the air, right past the open classroom door. Mr. Pellegrin watched as it landed perfectly on his desk. He did not raise his voice, but simply walked to the center of the classroom and asked who did it. We knew, but everyone sat in silence. He then told us that whoever did it was going to the boiler room. He also said that if no one came forward, the whole class would go to the boiler room.

I immediately went into a state of fear and trembling. I could not believe that Nick would not admit to doing this, or that no one else in the class would speak up. Why couldn't there have been at least one person to speak up and deliver the class from such a terrible situation?

Being the brave hero that I am, I knew it was time for me to step forward. At the last minute, right before the whole class was to get up and head to the boiler room, I raised my hand. Mr. Pellegrin automatically assumed that my upraised hand was my admission that I was the guilty party and willing to take my punishment for the sake of the class. I quickly assured Mr. Pellegrin that that was not my intention, and that I was not guilty. I did not make the airplane and I did not sail it onto his desk. With daring confidence, boldness, and fearlessness, I declared, unwaveringly, that it was Nick who did it.

Nick Orange quickly replied, "It wasn't me, it was Yankee."

Without any hesitation, Mr. Pellegrin ordered us both to the boiler room. I could not believe this was really happening. This was before I ever heard of *The Twilight Zone*. I remember standing to the side and watching as Nick was asked to drop his trousers. He was then asked to bend over and grab his ankles. Nick began to whimper as soon as he saw the size of that paddle and knew what was coming. When contact was made, Nick must have come a foot off the floor. When my moment of truth came, I knew it was not going to end well. It's never easy walking back into a classroom with all the kids staring at you and watching as you try to sit down on a blistered rear-end. Why did everything always have to happen to me?

Yankee and the Flying Jenny

Our closest neighbors lived about a half-mile away. Sometimes, we would go to their house and play on their Flying Jenny. The Flying Jenny is a pretty simple thing, made of two logs with a spike holding them together. It's like a big seesaw that spins around. It works best when you have two people standing on the ground next to the people sitting on the seats. Those that are standing push the Jenny as fast as they can. Of course, those that are riding enjoy it much more than those that are pushing, so everybody takes turns. It was very easy to fall off and get hurt, but thankfully, very few did—until one day when my sisters Net and Kay were the riders, and I was the one pushing.

Everything was going along fine until Net decided to jump off. Automatically, Net's side of the log went up, and Kay's side of the log went down. The Flying Jenny landed on me and folded me up under the heavy log. When they lifted the log off me, it was easily noticeable that my left arm looked very funny. I did not know until later that my arm was broken in four places between my elbow and my wrist.

The Pearson children ran to tell their mother what had happened. We knew that they were a religious family because, on occasion, we heard them talk about God, and heard them pray. When their mother saw me, she picked me up (I was only about five or six years old) and began to pray, out loud, for a doctor. Here we were way out in the woods, on dirt roads, with no one else around and probably twenty miles from Athens, Georgia. I'll never forget her carrying me down to the crossroads and looking both ways. There were no vehicles coming or going, and she prayed to the Lord to send us a doctor immediately.

As we looked way down the road that ran past our house, we saw dust, and then a car. When the car got to the crossroads, everybody started flagging it down so it would stop. This man got out and Mrs. Pearson explained to him why I urgently needed to be taken to the hospital. Would you believe it, this man was a doctor? He quickly put two pieces of wood on either side of my arm and wrapped it with gauze. After I trusted Christ later in life, I came to believe, for reasons unknown to me, that God has watched over me my whole life.

I never played on a Flying Jenny again.

Little Man vs Big Man

or

THE CHIHUAHUA TAKES ON THE ROTTWEILER

I f you're going to have a little brother, you may as well go ahead and have one like I have. His nickname is Little Man. When he was small, it didn't seem like he was ever going to grow. He could walk when he was seven months old and run when he was nine months old.

My dad with me and Little Man

There are not too many stories about me and my little brother, because there is a four-year age difference between us. But this is one story I will never forget. We were living in the Parkview Apartments in Athens, Georgia, in 1959. On a hill behind our apartment was a youth center where children from the community would get together. I was asked to be the youth director, to plan and engage the teenagers in various activities. I was not saved during this time, so there was nothing spiritual about the things we did. We decided to have a dance night, various activities, and cold drinks in the center's rec room. The total price was ten cents a person. Everyone seemed to be enjoying themselves, and I spent time with Betty, my newfound girlfriend.

It wasn't long, though, before this young boy, who might've been about eleven or twelve, came over to me and informed me that another boy was bullying him, and he wanted me to stop it.

Of course, this seemed like no big deal. Music was playing, but nobody was dancing. People were just standing around talking to each other. When I approached this young bully, I informed him that he must stop bullying the younger kid or he would have to leave the youth meeting. He said he understood, and that there would be no problem, so I went back to spend time with Betty.

Later, some of the kids came up to me to let me know that the bully was going to get his big brother to take care of me. Of course, I had never seen his big brother, so I wasn't worried; I told the kids not to be afraid, and that everything would be fine. Then I heard that the big brother had arrived. He was outside and was coming in to see me. I did notice that the outside streetlight, which was shining in through the window, was temporarily blocked by a pretty good-sized individual. This did cause me some concern.

Into the rec room walked William. He was big, strong, and fearsome. I found out later that he had just gotten out of prison, working on the rock pile. He was also two years older than me. I was not that worried because I knew two mature adults like William and I could very easily settle a problem between two young kids.

When I walked over to him, I had to look up. That's when I noticed his massive arms and shoulders and realized that this might not end very well. He quickly wanted to know where this Yankee fellow was who had picked on his little brother and threatened to throw him out of the recreation center. We settled into a non-threatening discussion about what had happened. Eventually he felt pretty confident that the issue was settled, and that no harm was done or meant.

That was when my little brother got involved. If you have ever seen a little Chihuahua walking up to a Rottweiler, and barking profusely without understanding the seriousness of his predicament, then you will better understand what it was like for my little brother to get in the face of William. There was absolutely no doubt that my little brother meant well, but to him rules are rules. Since William had not paid his dime to come into the rec center, my brother informed me, and all the kids in the room, that it was my duty to kick him out unless he paid his dime. I turned to my brother and told him that William did not have to pay the dime, and that there was no problem because he was going to leave.

Evidently, Little Man did not hear a word that I said.

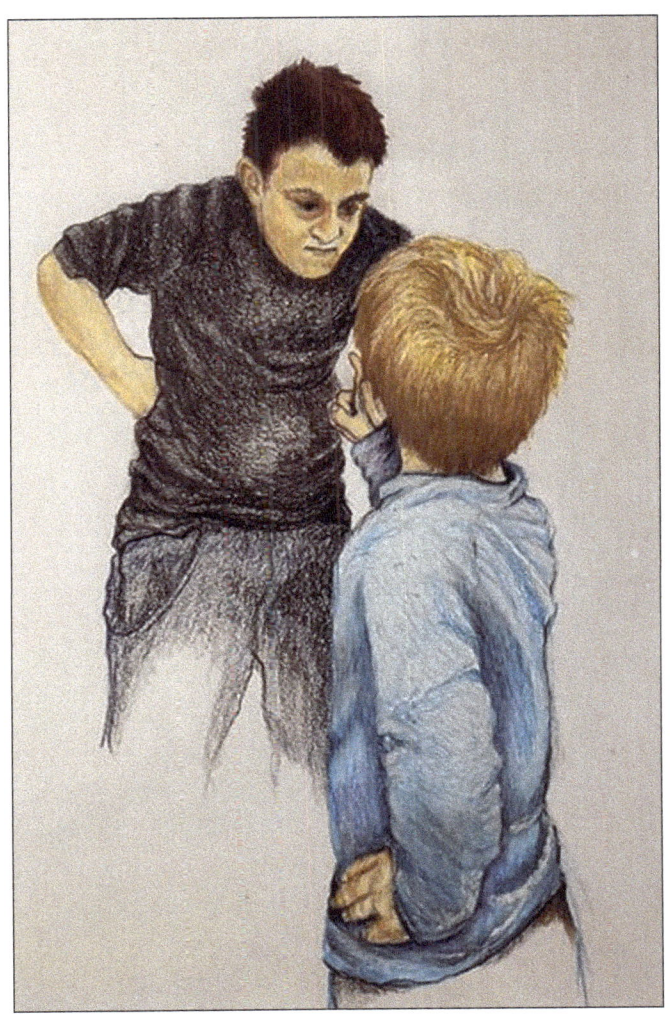

My brother pointed his finger toward William's face and charged me before all to throw him out. At this point, William had had enough. He grabbed Little Man by the shirt, and with one arm lifted him clean off the floor. He drew back his right hand and was about to totally anni-hilate my little brother when I, being the hero that I am, jumped into action. I hit William, and I hit him, and I hit him. And then I hit the floor. We both wound up falling to the floor when I heard a kid standing nearby saying, "Yankee, your nose looks funny." I quickly moved my hand to the middle of my face to touch my nose. It was not there; it had been moved to the left side of my face.

Before William could get up from the floor, Bruce Lee—I mean my brother, Little Man—had taken a metal chair and brought it down upon William's head. About this time the police arrived. I was taken to the hospital with a broken nose, and the next day to the courthouse. No charges were pressed. William and I were never close friends, but neither were we enemies.

A Knife in the Foot

One could say I was a bit of an adventuresome child, fantasizing about the days when the cowboys and Indians roamed the West. I remember bringing home two books that I got from the school library. One was about Daniel Boone, and the other was about Davy Crockett. I could picture myself reliving the events written about their lives. On many occasions, I would walk into the woods carrying a hatchet and a throwing knife, which I would practice throwing by the hours. I thought I had gotten pretty good. I just knew that I had been born at the wrong time.

Maybe you never heard of the game called splits. Back then almost every boy who carried a pocketknife was willing to take on all challengers in the wonderful game of splits. The game is simple: a boy would face his challenger with both feet together. The goal was to throw your knife to the outside of either of the other boy's feet so that the knife stuck in the ground no more than six inches from either foot Then the boy receiving the throw was required to move his foot against the knife blade. It was then his turn to throw.

The goal was to keep extending the other boy's feet further and further apart until they either split their britches, fell down, or could no longer stretch. My friend who lived up the road and I were engaged in a very exciting match, when I threw my knife right into his shoe.

The blade not only pierced the leather on the top of his shoe, but also went into his foot. When he stopped rolling on the ground and crying out in pain, he got up and hobbled to his house, which was just across the street.

Now, you and I know it was an honest mistake—an accident that could've happened to anybody. That wasn't conveyed when he told his mother what I did.

My mother was alerted and came running to the neighbor's house to see what her son had done this time. I don't understand why my mother was not more understanding. She beat the tar out of me. There was a lesson to be learned. I never played splits again.

A BB in the Eye

❖

When my Uncle Merle lived in a little town called Hunterdale, Virginia, he bought me a little BB gun so that I could enjoy shooting at rabbits and squirrels in the woods behind the house. It was kind of out in the country without too many neighbors around.

Several of the boys in the area decided to build us a treehouse for boys only. Since all of us owned our own BB guns, we thought it could be fun to choose sides and pretend to have a gunfight between the good guys and the bad guys. Some would be in the treehouse, and the rest would hide behind trees. No one was to deliberately try to shoot at anyone's head because it was all just in fun. We had done this before using slingshots. As far as I know, no one ever got hurt.

We were having a great time until I shot into the window of the treehouse. It was dark inside the treehouse, and I saw no one, but thought I would take a chance and try to hit someone. I will never forget the scream. I heard this boy yelling at the top of his lungs that somebody had shot him in the eye. We all stopped firing and ran up to the treehouse. This boy came running out with his hand over his right eye, heading home as fast as he could run.

They all knew that it was me who fired the shot. All the kids immediately disbanded and went home. It is very difficult to state how I felt. I knew I had just put out a boy's eye; I was so afraid of what was going to happen. I did not know if his parents were coming to the house to see my aunt and uncle. I didn't know how badly his eye was hurt, or how my relatives were going to take this, or what they would do to me. The suspense was too much. I did not tell them what had happened because I did not know if they would put me in a home or send me to jail; I couldn't stand it. It was one long, torturous night, but when daylight finally came, I ventured outside.

It seemed impossible, but the boy that I shot with my BB gun was walking down the street. I did not know whether to run and hide, or stand still and face the music. When he got close to me, he looked straight at me with both eyes and a smile on his face and asked me how I was doing. It blew me away when he told me that his eye was fine, and it wasn't hurting anymore. I do not know if he ever told his mom and dad, but I was so thrilled that he was not blind. I asked him where I hit him. He pulled the bottom of his eyelid down to show me the spot. The BB was still there. With great care, I got the BB out of his eye.

I never again shot a BB gun at anyone. Some people live and learn, and some people live and never learn. At this rate, I should be the smartest man in the world.

Yankee and Robin Hood

❖

One of my favorite childhood stories was Robin Hood splitting an arrow. From a considerable distance away, Robin Hood could shoot an arrow into a bull's-eye, and then split that arrow with another arrow.

Now I am going to tell you a story I know you will find hard to believe, but it's true. Were there witnesses to this dramatic feat of mine? No, but it is the truth. I got two bales of hay and placed them at the end of our yard. I put a target on one bale, got my bow, and shot my arrow into the bale of hay. I was so proud that I hit the bull's-eye, but disappointed that no one saw it. When I removed my arrow, I noticed that the little metal tip on the end of the arrow was missing. I thought it might have dropped on the ground when I removed the arrow from the hay bale, but I could not find it.

As I remember, I only had about three arrows. I was fearful about missing the bale of hay and having the arrow slide along the ground, hiding itself in the grass where I had lost arrows before.

I shot another arrow at the target. Would you believe that I shot another bull's-eye? When I removed my arrow, I did so slowly and carefully so as not to lose another little metal tip. There, on the end of my second arrow, was the metal tip from my first one, the tip that I believed I'd lost. I thought to myself, *Yankee, you just shot as good as Robin Hood himself!* But there was no one around. I just had to tell someone what I had done. I took my trusty bow, and the couple of arrows that were left, and walked up the road to see a friend of mine. I don't know if he believed me. I had to demonstrate just how good I was. I really don't remember what I was going to shoot at, but I shot an arrow into the air, and where it went, I knew not where. My friend then informed me that my arrow had stuck in the top of a tree. I could not afford to lose that arrow.

The only way I could get that arrow was to climb the tree. So, up the tree I went. I knew I would have to hug some of those limbs, but I didn't want to get my shirt dirty or torn. I took it off. When I got to where I could reach my arrow, I did not notice the live power lines that were going through the tree.

When I leaned back to get the arrow, my sweaty back touched the live wires. The jolt knocked me up against the tree. For a brief moment, I could not move and was kind of frozen to the tree. My friend rounded up a couple of adult men who climbed up and helped me get down. When they looked at my back, they found two little black holes. They were not too deep, but they were the spot where the live wire burned me. The men could not believe that I had lived. I never did figure out how that arrow got up into that tree, especially when I was as good as I was.

Lizzie Saves My Life

When my sister Lizzie and I were living in Hunterdale, Virginia, we decided to go swimming in the river with several other friends whose names I no longer recall. I was not a good swimmer, so I simply waded in the water next to the bank. Lizzie was a great swimmer, with terrific form and style. Everyone was impressed with how well she could dive off that high tree limb and swim back to the bank.

I guess you could call it being jealous of my sister, but I determined that if she could do it, I could do it. I got everyone's attention so that they would watch me climb that tree, get out on that limb, dive into the water, and swim back to the bank. My sister made it look so easy, so I knew it could not be very hard. When I got out on the limb, however, I could not believe how scared I was, or how far the water was from the limb.

The water, being a little murky, made it virtually impossible to see the bottom of the river. No one had ever told me that I needed to turn my hands up when I hit the water so that I would quickly return to the surface. I could not tell how my sister did it; I only saw her put one hand on top of the other and point them toward the water. I thought you would just come up automatically. I remember standing on the limb and telling everyone, "Watch! I am going to do it!" This was really a great moment in my life. Although I was scared, I dove toward the water.

I went through the air without any problem. I went through the water without any problem. But I did not come up. I went straight to the bottom where my head went almost a foot into the mud. Sharp pains went through the left side of my head, my neck, and down my back. I was totally shocked. Have you ever had your foot stuck in the mud where the suction made it almost impossible to lift your foot? Try that with your head while it's stuck in the mud at the bottom of a river.

When I finally got my head unstuck, I remember slowly rising to the surface as if in a dream. My sister Lizzie got into the water and brought me to the riverbank. At this point in my life, I did not know that being a showoff was not a sign of virtue.

How Not to Catch a Wabbit

❖

My dad not only made moonshine, but he also drank a lot of it. He never let us see where his liquor still was, but my mother would often go and get the corn mash used in making moonshine and bring it home for us kids to eat. We were poor, but we didn't know it because nobody told us. My mother would make big pans of biscuits, and while they were piping hot, we would take black molasses, butter, or peanut butter, and stir it up real good, then sop it up with the biscuits. It was one of my favorite meals. Another one of my favorite meals was hot, crumbled-up cornbread in a glass with ice cold buttermilk. To me, this was better than ice cream. But my all-time favorite was rabbit stew.

My dad had five rabbit boxes scattered around the woods that kept us in a lot of rabbit stew. It was Lizzie and Net's responsibility to check the rabbit boxes. I was considered too young to go into the woods or handle the rabbits. I begged my two sisters to let me go; I told them I would not say anything or do anything wrong. I just wanted to watch.

I was so excited when they said I could go with them to look for rabbits.

When we got to the first rabbit box, the stick inside had been triggered, and the door to the box was shut. We knew that a rabbit had been caught. Lizzie pulled up the door, reached in, and pulled out the rabbit. I pleaded with them to let me hold the rabbit, promising that I would not let it get away. My request was denied, and the rabbit was given to Net. At the second rabbit box, Lizzie reached in and got the rabbit, and once again, I pleaded with them to let me hold the rabbit and promised that I would not let it get away, but the answer was the same. So now, Lizzie and Net were each walking through the woods holding a rabbit. When we got to the third rabbit box we knew we were going to have three rabbits. I was sure that I was going to get to hold a rabbit, but once again, Lizzie said no. She walked over to a tree and beat the tree several times with the head of the rabbit.

The rabbit wasn't moving, so she laid it down at the trunk of the tree. She then reached in and got the third rabbit, and when she did, we all noticed that the rabbit by the tree had come back to life and had started hopping away.

At the same moment, Lizzie and Net threw down the rabbits they were holding and started after the rabbit that was hopping away. In less than a minute, we had lost three rabbits. I don't remember us ever checking the last two boxes, but I do remember that when we got home it was all my fault that we lost all three rabbits. My sisters had done it to me again. I do not remember ever going with them to check the rabbit boxes again.

The Day I Lost My Marbles

B ack in the early fifties, it was only normal for all the boys to have a pocketknife and a few marbles in their pocket. When you have marbles, you can play anywhere and anytime. All you needed was a circle on some dirt and you were ready to go.

Everyone would use regular sized marbles. Cat's eye marbles were the common favorite. Each person would put the same number of marbles within the circle. You could shoot at any marble as long as your shooting hand was outside the circle. You got to keep whatever marble you hit that went outside the circle. To determine who got to go first, we would simply draw a line, and everyone would pitch a marble to that line; the closest to the line would go first. During the game, if you shot without knocking a marble outside the circle, you lost your turn.

Although on occasion I would win a few marbles, I never got to clean house, and sometimes I even lost all my marbles. The boys would love to come in from recess with their pockets bulging with marbles. This was the evidence that someone was good. Only one time was I on a roll; and I got to keep shooting because I kept knocking marbles out of the circle. You've never seen such an excited, happy kid as me. My two front pockets were so full of marbles that I had trouble walking.

With my last name being Arnold, I usually sat toward the front of the class. This day, after recess (and my great marble shooting achievement), I sat down, stretched out my legs, crossed my feet, and leaned way back in my seat. That is when I realized I had made a serious blunder.

I did not see it at first, but I heard marbles hitting the floor and rolling down both aisles toward the back of the classroom. It did not take the teacher long to approach me and confiscate all of my marbles. I never got them back. A day of jubilation ended in total despair for me. As I recall, I never again played marbles at school.

What Did Yankee Hear That Totally Changed His Destiny and His Life?

❖

Friend, let me tell you the best news I ever heard. A few months after I quit school at seventeen, ran away from home, and joined the Navy,, I heard the greatest love story ever told. The Bible says that we are all sinners and that no one is perfect but God. The Word of God tells us that the wages of sin is death—meaning eternal separation from God—in a literal fire burning hell. *Just hearing that was enough to scare me to death.*

God says that heaven is a perfect place, and we need to be as righteous as God to go there. Because of sin we cannot get in. *If this was true, my chances of going to heaven looked pretty slim.*

The Lord tells us that no man can save himself by his good works. The Bible says, in Ephesians 2:8 and 9, "For by grace are ye saved through faith; and that not of yourselves: it is the gift of God: Not of works, lest any man should boast." Heaven is not a reward for living right. It cannot be earned by anything we could say or do. *This was the first time I heard that going to heaven was free.*

God loved us so much that He sent His son Jesus Christ into the world to pay for not only *my* sins, but the sins of the whole world. He loves you but He hates your sins because they separate you from God. *This was new to me; I did not know that God loved me.* He died on the cross to make a complete payment for all sins, for all time, and for all people. He came back again from the dead and will save anyone who believes He did it for them.

The very moment you believe that Christ did this for you, He puts the death payment He made to your account and promises you the free gift of eternal life. He promises that He will never cast you out or lose you. The Word of God says in I John 5:13, "These things have I written unto you that believe on the name of the son of God, which is Jesus Christ, that ye may know that ye have (that means right now) Eternal Life" (parentheses mine).

Friend, if that makes sense to you, would you right now do what I did over sixty years ago, just the best you know how, and trust Jesus Christ to take you to heaven whenever you die? What a wonderful joy to know that I am forgiven by God and will spend eternity with Him in heaven. Will you join me?

Thanks for reading my little journey through time. Hope you were blessed. Yankee Arnold.

If you enjoyed, **share!**

Yankee Arnold Ministries
7028 W. Waters Ave Suite 316
Tampa, Florida, 33634
Yankee@YankeeArnold.com

CPSIA information can be obtained
at www.ICGtesting.com
Printed in the USA
LVHW070030031121
702253LV00018B/2188